IMAGES OF ENGLAND

CAMDEN TOWN AND KENTISH TOWN

IMAGES OF ENGLAND

CAMDEN TOWN
AND
KENTISH TOWN

MARIANNE COLLOMS AND
DICK WEINDLING

The
History
Press

Regent's Park Barracks, Albany Street, c. 1897. A parade of the Lifeguards and the Queen's Trumpeters (in the foreground). A resident who lived nearby recalled guardsmen hiring his father's cart to transport families and household goods to and from Windsor Castle. Soldiers turned out to help with local incidents, including an explosion on the canal and a fire at Camden Town railway yard. The barracks were also mentioned in H.G. Wells' novel *The War of the Worlds*, in which several scenes were set locally.

Frontispiece: William Doughty, builder, 107 Kentish Town Road, 1903. The plaque gives the old name of this terrace between Clarence and Castle Roads as Providence Place, built in 1819. Doughty took over an existing business in the 1890s, and in 1901 was living over the shop with his family. The firm continued trading until the mid-1930s and although the plaque has gone, the building still stands.

First published in 2003 by Tempus Publishing

Reprinted in 2009 by
The History Press
The Mill, Brimscombe Port,
Stroud, Gloucestershire, GL5 2QG
www.thehistorypress.co.uk

Reprinted 2011

© Marianne Colloms and Dick Weindling, 2009

The right of Marianne Colloms and Dick Weindling to be identified as
the Author of this work has been asserted in accordance with the
Copyrights, Designs and Patents Act 1988.

British Library Cataloguing in Publication Data.
A catalogue record for this book is available from the British Library.

ISBN 978 0 7524 2922 9

Typesetting and origination by Tempus Publishing
Printed and bound in England.

Contents

Acknowledgements

Special thanks are due to the staff of the Camden Local Studies and Archives Centre, in particular Mark Aston, Aidan Flood, Malcolm Holmes, Richard Knight and Lesley Marshall, for their continuing help and co-operation. Thanks are also due Emily Brand, BAT; Michael Goodall; Hannah Kay, Rhodes Museum Curator; Susanna Lamb, Madame Tussaud's archive; Dermot Morrin OP, St Dominic's Priory; David Ruddom, volunteer research consultant, London Transport Museum; Bill Slaughter, LDS Archive, Salt Lake City; David Stevens, Company Archivist, J. Sainsbury plc; Karen Thompson, Salvation Army International Headquarters.

Every effort has been made to contact the owners of the images reproduced in this book. All illustrations are copyright and reproduced with the kind permission of the following: The London Borough of Camden: Cover; Doughty p.2; Fort & Lord Camden p.10; Bateman house & Kentish Town view p.11; Mother Damnable & Toll house p.12; Farmhouse & Kentish Town view p.13; Agar Town p.14; Inwood Place p.15; Oakley Square p.18; H.G. Wells p.19; Yuri Gargarin p.24; church p.27; chapel & church p.29; chapel & church p.30; horses p.35; Colonel Jack & duel p.36; train crash p.37; Finch murder p.38; Camden Town murder p.39; bomb damage p.43; factory p.45; Gilbey property p.47; Brewery & Rowneys p.48; St Pancras Wells p.52; Cooke's Cirque p.53; Tavern p.54; Sayers' portrait and funeral p.55; Park Theatre p.56; Camden Theatre p.57; Bedford Theatre p.58; Sickert p.59; Plaza p.60; programme p.61; acrobats p.62; Wally Pone p.64; two images, Royal Veterinarian College p.67; Exhibition p.69; Goldington Buildings & Rowton House p.71; Fountain p.72; Statue & Library p.73; Cobden p.74; Boys' Home pp.75 & 80; Dame School & Academy p.76; Drawing School p.77; Governess Asylum p.78; Camden Town Schools p.79; University p.83; class photo p.85; leaflet p.86; chemist p.88; Inverness Street p.91; Camden High Street p.94; Oetzmann p.96; Bull & Gate p.99; Tally Ho p.101; Red Cap p.102; Rayners p.105; Beddalls p.106; Daniels p.107; Arnold p.108; Barley p.109; Salmon & Gluckstein p.110; Birdseye p.111; Dairy & Merralls p.112; Cossor p.115; adverts p.116; shed p.117; Bridge p.118; Camden Lock p.119; dairy p.120; Roundhouse p.122; Station & Pickford's Depot p.123; tram p.127, bus p.128.

Marianne Colloms: Barracks p.4; Mornington Crescent p.18; church p.28; Crippen house p.41; bed p.49; Doris Keane p.57; Bale p.59; Forum p.61; Lido p.63; class photo p.79; building p.80; Working Men's College p.83; Holy Rood House p.85; Wellington Street p.91; Camden Road p.101; Dublin Castle p.102; Kentish Town Road pp.106 & 108; Sibley p.110; canal and horse barge p.118. All images on pages 17, 20-23, 25-26, 31-34, 46, 50, 65, 66, 68, 70, 81-82, 84, 89, 90, 92-93, 95, 97, 98, 103,114, 121, 124, 125 and 126.

Bishop's Stortford Museum, Gilbey Archive: packers p.47.
Charles Goodall & Son Ltd: factory p.49.
Henry Grant Collection, Museum of London: rent strike demonstration p.43; Enosis demonstration p.44; Lamp post game p.63; taxidermist p.87.
J. Sainsbury's archive: three Sainsbury stores in Kentish Town & Queens Crescent pp. 111 & 113.
Madame Tussaud's archive: advert p.42.

Introduction

Originally the adjacent districts of Kentish Town and Camden Town lay in the parish (later the Borough) of St Pancras. Today this forms part of the larger London Borough of Camden.

Kentish and Camden Towns developed along two main roads that led north from central London to the villages of Hampstead and Highgate. The road to Highgate passed by the parish church of St Pancras. The earliest settlement in the area was established nearby, on the banks of the Fleet river. A second group of houses developed further north, near the present junction of Royal College Street and Kentish Town Road. This became the village of Kentish Town and a straggling line of houses grew up on either side of the main road. The village provided an attractive country retreat for wealthy Londoners, and several large mansions were built, especially on the more northerly stretch of road to Highgate. While the village of Kentish Town prospered and a local chapel was built in 1456, the area around St Pancras parish church suffered a general decline.

In the early nineteenth century, the local fields were mainly meadowland, harvested for hay or grazed by cattle. Thomas Rhodes, an ancestor of the explorer Cecil Rhodes, farmed a large part of the neighbourhood.

Unlike its neighbour, 'Camden Town' did not exist until local landowner Lord Camden obtained a 1791 Act of Parliament to grant building leases for his property east of Camden High Street. Before that date, there were only open fields, with scattered houses, inns and cottages along the few roads. In 1821 a second Act of Parliament authorised the building of Camden Road, northwest to Holloway. Other landowners soon followed Lord Camden's example and started to develop their property. Lord Southampton owned most of the land on the west side of Camden High Street as far as Chalk Farm. This was the name given to the area at the foot of Primrose Hill, north of Camden Town. Apart from a few cottages, for many years the main building here was a tavern, much visited by Londoners in search of rural amusements.

As the nineteenth century progressed, builders created a network of streets and lined most of the new roads with terraced houses or semi-detached villas. These aimed at attracting the middle classes, but some districts, for example, certain streets in Gospel Oak, catered for a less prosperous class of tenant.

A large number of public houses were built along the main roads. Some date back to the eighteenth century and are still in existence today. For example, The Bull and Gate, Kentish Town and the Chalk Farm Tavern appear in records of 1721 and 1732 respectively, but were probably in existence before that. Today the neighbourhood still supports many pubs, some well known as live music venues.

As the nineteenth-century streets filled with houses and tenants, so new churches were built to cater for their spiritual needs. An increasing number of Nonconformist sects also established places of worship in both neighbourhoods. As with many metropolitan districts, changes in population structure have since led to some churches and chapels falling into disrepair. A number have been demolished, while others have been adapted to serve new faiths or secular pursuits.

Many early schools were private and exclusively for boys. The 1870 Education Act provided education for all and a number of large School Board buildings were built in both neighbourhoods.

Camden Town and Chalk Farm experienced some of London's major transport innovations. In 1820 the Grand Junction Canal was opened. The main waterway passed through Regent's Park to Camden Town and on to the Thames at Limehouse. In 1837 the London & Birmingham Railway Co. began running trains through Camden Town to their London terminus at Euston.

Two more railway companies laid tracks across the fields of Kentish Town in the 1850s and 1860s. Houses in their path had to be demolished while others ended up sandwiched tight against the railway viaduct. On the roads, horse buses were joined by trams and later replaced by motor and trolley buses. Today the local authorities are attempting to ease traffic congestion by providing dedicated bus and bike lanes, and there are suggestions that parts of the busy Camden High Street should be closed to vehicles, at least at the weekends.

Amusements were simple, such as outings to the Adam and Eve tea gardens near Old St Pancras Church. Inns such as the Chalk Farm Tavern regularly laid on entertainment, and Camden Town was later home to one of London's leading variety venues, the Bedford Music Hall. Music hall gave way to the cinema, but of the many that were opened in the neighbourhood, just one working cinema remains in business today.

The availability of land attracted philanthropic institutions to the area, while inner London parishes acquired plots for new burial grounds. Industry was drawn to the streets near the railway lines and provided much local employment, as did the railways themselves. The area became a noted centre of the piano-making industry. The main roads – Camden High Street and Kentish Town Road – developed into prime shopping areas, supplying most of the needs of the householders in the neighbouring residential streets. Today the sale of large tracts of railway sidings has permitted the development of new commercial estates and superstores. The markets in and around Camden Lock have become the second most popular tourist attraction in London, attracting millions of visitors each year.

In the years immediately preceding the Second World War, Camden and Kentish Towns suffered a general decline. Many of the original family-owned houses had been converted into flats or bedsits and become overcrowded and run down. The Councils of St Pancras, and later Camden, embarked on redevelopment schemes that eradicated entire neighbourhoods, replacing old terraces with new accommodation, largely taking the form of blocks of flats. For example, Maitland Park, an area of comfortable villa residences off Haverstock Hill, along with nearby streets centred on Lismore Circus in Gospel Oak, were all demolished. Much of southern Camden Town on either side of the Hampstead Road, formed another major area of redevelopment. In post-war years, Irish and later Greek-Cypriot communities established themselves in Camden Town. Today both it and neighbouring Kentish Town are busy cosmopolitan neighbourhoods, with a constant turnover of commercial premises. Good road, rail and tube links have helped promote their popularity as residential districts.

One

Early Days

This very rural scene shows the Fleet river in 1825 near St Pancras. The Fleet, once a major waterway, still flows from two sources on Hampstead Heath. Now underground, the eastern section begins in the grounds of Kenwood and creates the chain of Highgate ponds, while the western arm starts near the Vale of Health and forms the Hampstead ponds. The two arms joined north of Camden Town (near today's Hawley Road) and passed under Kentish Town Road flowing south towards St Pancras. From here the Fleet went to Holborn and eventually into the Thames at Blackfriars. Sadly, this once pleasant river became so smelly and polluted that it was covered over. It is still used as a sewer today.

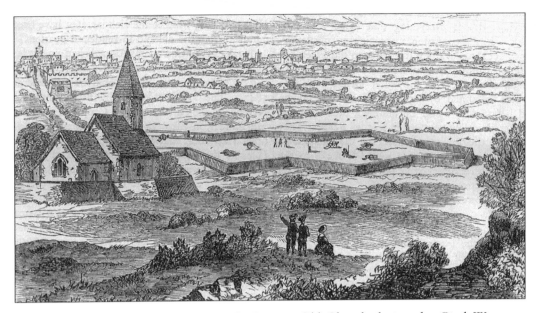

This view, showing fortifications near St Pancras Old Church during the Civil War, was originally thought to date from 1642. At the time, a number of forts were built to guard London against Royalist attack. In November, fifty Parliamentarian soldiers were billeted in the church. However, recent research indicates the engraving is a forgery, and no defences were built on this site.

An engraving of Charles Pratt, the first Earl of Camden (1713-1794) who was a major local landowner. Building began on his property in 1791, and he lent his name to the resulting development of Camden Town. Family connections are reflected by street names such as 'Greenland', who was Camden's builder, 'Georgiana', one of his daughters and 'Jeffrey's', his wife's maiden name.

Pictured in 1787, soon after it was completed, Kentish Town House faced Highgate Road. It was built by London solicitor Gregory Bateman, and included an ornamental water garden, fed by the River Fleet. Building costs ruined the lawyer and the house was nicknamed 'Bateman's Folly'. Today, St Albans Road stands on the site.

The junction of Royal College Street (left) and Kentish Town Road, looking south, 1772. Unrecognizable today, this rural view is by Swiss painter Samuel Hieronymus Grimm. Directions 'To Gray's Inn' and 'To St Giles' are painted on the house at the road fork. The Black Horse pub with its swinging sign is on the left, in the direction of Gray's Inn. In the 1860s the landlady was fond of a pipe of tobacco and kept a pig as a companion in her back parlour.

Mother Damnable
of KENTISH TOWN
Anno 1676.

Sometimes associated with the Mother Red Cap pub at Camden Town, this strange looking woman was known as 'Mother Damnable' or 'the shrew of Kentish Town'; legend names her as Jinney Bingham. At the time of the Civil War she lived with a number of men, several of who died in suspicious circumstances. In old age she was a fortune-teller and a healer of strange diseases, but locals called her a witch. She wore a red cap and the black patches on her clothes were thought to be flying bats.

Toll house, Camden Town, c. 1860. Turnpike Trusts maintained certain roads in nineteenth-century London; gates were placed across the roadway and traffic paid to pass through. This toll house was located where the Cobden statue now stands opposite Mornington Crescent station, and was removed in 1864. Incredibly, the photograph was taken using a spectacle glass for a lens and a cigar box for a camera.

This is part of a panorama of Kentish Town, drawn by John King, c. 1850. The large house on the left was St John's farmhouse. Mr Minshull, a magistrate, previously occupied this property with its nineteen acres of land. The house was demolished after the railway was built in the 1860s, and Denyer House now occupies the site.

Another pen drawing by Grimm in 1772, this time looking north from the junction of today's Royal College Street and Kentish Town Road. The inn on the left is the Castle Tavern, which had tea gardens that reached down to the banks of the Fleet.

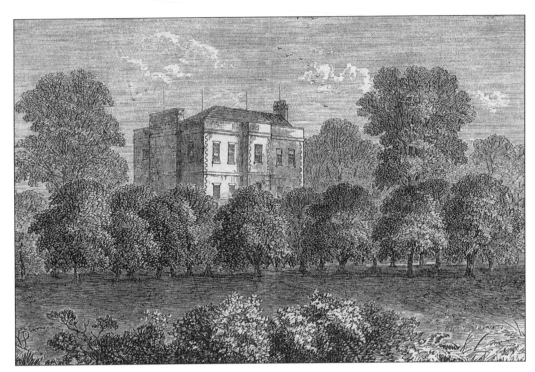

In 1810, lawyer William Agar built Elm Lodge, a substantial house in the fields north of the St Pancras Old Church. The house was surrounded by mulberry trees with tall poplars along its boundaries. Agar subsequently attempted to stop the Regent's Canal from crossing his property. He failed, but won handsome financial compensation. Elm Lodge was demolished by the Midland Railway Co. in 1867.

Paradise Row, Agar Town, 1853. In the 1840s William Agar's descendants leased land behind St Pancras Old Church to developers who built Agar Town, an area of working-class housing. It was certainly a poor district but conditions were exaggerated by contemporary reports. Agar Town lay in the path of the Midland Railway line to St Pancras and was demolished in 1866.

Two

Home Sweet Home

Kentish Town Road looking north, prior to 1868. This early photograph shows the Assembly House pub, the low white building at the corner of Leighton Road. By 1868 the Midland Railway station had replaced Montague Place (immediately south of Leighton Road), while the adjoining houses of Inwood Place were converted into shops. They were later absorbed into the site of Kentish Town Underground station.

Charles Dickens lived at several addresses in the area, although all the houses have since been demolished. In 1822, when he was ten, the family moved from Chatham to No. 16 (renumbered as 141) Bayham Street, now marked by a plaque. Charles was unhappy here; the family lived under cramped conditions and soon afterwards Dickens' father was sent to Marshalsea prison for debt. When things improved, in 1825 the family moved to 29 Johnson Street (later Cranleigh Street), in Somers Town. Dickens used his recollections of the neighbourhood for scenes in his novels, notably the building of the London and Birmingham Railway through Camden Town. In 1858, after he separated from his wife Catherine, she moved to 70 Gloucester Crescent. A year later, Dickens' mistress, Ellen Ternan (known as Nelly), moved into 2 Houghton Place (off Ampthill Square), which Dickens may have purchased for her.

Ampthill Square, *c.* 1900. Built round an oval-shaped central garden, bisected by the railway into Euston, attempts were made to stop locomotives from smoking and annoying residents. The boy in the background is pushing his friend in a homemade cart – a wooden packing case on pram wheels. These houses were demolished in the 1960s and replaced by a housing estate.

Crowndale Road junction with College Place, *c.* 1910. Renamed in 1863, Crowndale Road was originally 'Fig Lane'. The houses shown have been demolished, apart from the Church Hall, to the left of the tree. Built in 1897, it currently houses Theatro Technis, a Greek-Cypriot theatre. The recently-completed Working Men's College with its cupola is in the background.

Oakley Square, shown here before its entry gates were removed in 1893. These stopped all through traffic, in contrast to today's fast traffic. The gatekeeper's lodge (shown in the centre) still stands at the end of the central garden. All the houses on the left, including No. 6 where Lenin was living in 1911, have been demolished, as has St Matthew's church opposite.

Mornington Crescent before its communal garden was built over in the 1920s. Eminent residents have included artist Walter Sickert (No. 6, marked with a blue plaque). In the 1850s, a school for the sons of missionaries occupied Nos 35 and 36 on the Arlington Road corner. Linked only at ground level, boys would crawl along a narrow roof ledge to move between dormitories!

H.G. Wells lodged with his aunt at 46 Fitzroy Road from 1889 to 1891 while he taught at Henley House School in Greville Road, Kilburn. In 1894 he went 'to live in sin and social rebellion' first at 7 Mornington Place, Hampstead Road, and then round the corner at 12 Mornington Terrace, with his mistress Catherine Robbins, whom he later married. Here he wrote *The Time Machine* and *The Island of Doctor Moreau*. In his later novel *The War of the Worlds*, Wells set one of the Martian strongholds on Primrose Hill, which he walked across each morning on his way to Kilburn.

Cambridge House, Regent's Park, with the buildings of Albany Street behind. The home of Camden Town distiller Sir Walter Gilbey, his 1901 household included no less than twenty-three servants! Before it became a private house, there was an adult orphan asylum on the site. In 1964 the house and land were redeveloped as the new Royal College of Physicians, designed by Sir Denys Lasdun.

Goldington Street, c. 1900. Looking towards the trees of Goldington Square, this terrace still stands at the junction with Platt Street. The corner premise was then a restaurant, advertising 'coffee and tea always ready', 'beefsteak pudding 4d'. This accounts for the carts; the drivers are enjoying a meal, as are their horses. Today it is a private house.

FRED. HONNOR,
Instrumentalist & Comedian.

LESSONS GIVEN ON THE BANJO & MANDOLINE.
Pianoforte Lessons by Miss LILY WALKER, CERT. T.C.M., L.C.M.
Address—5, ROCHESTER ROAD, CAMDEN ROAD, N.W.

Directories list the versatile Frederick Honnor as a teacher of music at No. 5 Rochester Road from around 1913 to 1923, when Miss Lily Walker took over. This was Fred's 'trade card', distributed in the hope of attracting both professional engagements and pupils.

Rochester Road, from a postcard sent in 1905. Houses on the Camden estate bordering Camden Road tended to be better quality compared with those further south, and attracted middle-class tenants such as self-employed businessmen. A block of local authority housing has replaced the attractive villas on the left, facing the communal garden.

Regent's Park Road, *c.* 1900. All these houses were probably the work of architect Henry Bassett. The Italianate pair with twin towers stood at the junction with Gloucester Avenue. They survived a demolition attempt in 1905, only to succumb after 1927. Cecil Sharp House, home of the English Folk Dance and Song Society, opened on their site in 1930.

This imposing terrace, Nos 72 to 94 Regent's Park Road, was demolished in 1963 and replaced by the Oldfield Estate. Note the large sunhats the boys are wearing. John Hayward Hawkins, owner of the priceless 'Witham Bowl', lived at No. 76. An outstanding example of Anglo-Saxon metalwork, the bowl disappeared without trace after his death in 1877.

In 1905, Annie, who lived at 70 Carlton Road, sent this card, showing the junction of her road with Queens Crescent, to her aunt. The recently-opened Turner's 'stewed eel and pie' shop was at 81 Carlton Road; the wall above displays adverts for Pears Soap, Birds Custard and local evening classes. The schoolboys probably attended nearby William Ellis School. The houses on the right were demolished in the 1960s.

Malden Road, looking south, between 1906 and 1908. The Ponsford Arms (with two roof urns) stood on the corner of Rhyl Street. The man in the doorway of No. 61 is wearing a striped apron, the trademark of a butcher. Henry Webb traded from here for fifty-nine years and the shop remained a butchers until 1964. Subsequent redevelopment has erased all the buildings on the right.

The Russian cosmonaut, Yuri Gagarin, in July 1961, saluting the grave of Karl Marx in Highgate Cemetery. Marx lived at several local addresses. In September 1856 he moved his family from Dean Street, Soho to 9 Grafton Terrace (currently No. 46). While living in Soho he produced the *Communist Manifesto* (1848) with Engels (who later lived at Nos 122 and 41 Regents Park Road). The influence of Marx's ideas has been enormous. His masterpiece, *Das Kapital*, called the 'Bible of the working class', was published in 1867 while he lived at No. 1 Maitland Park Road. His daughter described the house as 'a veritable palace and far too large and expensive'! In 1875 the family moved into nearby No. 41, where Marx died in 1883.

Posted in 1907, the message read 'you will see Eidy on her bike and her friend'. Maitland Park Road led to an enclave of comfortable villas. The Congregational church was used by children from the nearby Orphan School who nicknamed it 'Jack's Bakery' because it was so hot in summer. Along with all the Maitland Park houses, its site has since been redeveloped.

Clevedon Mansions, pre-First World War, one of several blocks of flats in Lissenden Gardens and immediate neighbourhood. Mansion blocks were one way of achieving maximum building value from a small site. In 1906, the poet John Betjeman was born in nearby Parliament Hill Mansions, and later described the 'red brick gloom' of this group of streets.

Mansfield Road Gospel Oak N. W.

Mansfield Road (left) and Lismore Road (right), with the distant trees of Lismore Circus. This photograph was taken soon after 1901, when the tramline crossing the foreground was opened along Agincourt Road. The imposing Mansfield Hotel was also a pub, rebuilt in the 1890s. Redevelopment has obliterated everything save the houses on the left.

In the 1960s and '70s, a combination of wartime bomb damage and run-down property persuaded the council to redevelop a large part of west Kentish Town, between Malden Road, Mansfield Road and Grafton Road. This block - 'Hawkridge' - is on Weedington Road.

Three

Spiritual Matters

St Pancras Old Church, 1815. Dating from before the Norman Conquest, this was the original parish church of St Pancras. Reports indicate the graveyard was in a worse condition than shown here. The isolated position in the open fields made it a target for the 'resurrection men', who dug up corpses to rob or sell them for dissection. In A *Tale of Two Cities* Charles Dickens describes a grave robbery here, calling the gruesome act 'going a fishing'.

OLD ST. PANCRAS CHURCH.

St Pancras Old Church, mid-1880s. To accommodate the growing number of worshippers, a new and much larger parish church was opened in 1822, on Euston Road. Among the many thousands of people interred in the burial grounds adjacent to the old church are the writer and pioneer feminist Mary Wollstonecraft; the unusual cross-dresser and French spy Chevalier d'Eon; the architect Sir John Soane and Captain John Mills, the last survivor of the Black Hole of Calcutta.

Jonathan Wild, on the way to his execution at Tyburn, 1725. Called 'The Great Thief-taker', Wild captured some notorious eighteenth-century villains, including Jack Sheppard. However, Wild played on both sides of the law, which eventually led to his downfall. Buried in the churchyard of St Pancras Old Church, the 'resurrection men' stole his body; his empty coffin was discovered nearby in Fig Lane, today's Crowndale Road.

Kentish Town chapel, Kentish Town Road, 1772. This was built to satisfy the requests of Kentish Town residents for a local place of worship, rather than undertaking the journey south, to the old parish church. In 1784, a new church on Highgate Road replaced the chapel, which was demolished. Eventually the site became part of C. & A. Daniels department store.

Opened in 1865, St Martin's, Vicars Road, was built at the personal cost of J.D. Allcroft to commemorate his wife. The first vicar had previously saved Allcroft's son from a lion attack in Africa. A listed building, today the church with its tall tower (minus the turret) stands in the middle of a modern housing estate. In the 1990s, the BBC soap *Eastenders* used the church for the wedding of Ricky and Bianca.

The Latter-Day Saints or Mormon chapel was in Royal College Street from 1854 to 1858. An 1849 newspaper reported that this sect was active in Camden Town and Somers Town. They were inviting people to emigrate to America, and live in farms near Salt Lake City.

St Paul's church, Camden Square, soon after opening in 1849. The location was given as 'Camden New Town', reflecting the fact that the streets on either side of Camden Road were just developing. This also explains the rural setting. St Paul's was demolished following bomb damage in the Second World War and replaced by a smaller building.

The banner reads 'Camden Wesleyan Sunday School, established 1862'. In 1860, the Wesleyans built a new chapel in Camden Street. The Whitsuntide crowd are dressed in their Sunday best, posing briefly for the photographer on a bridge, possibly over the Regent's Canal.

Consecrated in 1824, All Saints church, Camden Street was then described as 'neat and substantial'. The architects were William and Henry Inwood, who also designed the new St Pancras parish church. Closed in 1948, All Saints was subsequently taken over by the Greek Orthodox Church to serve the needs of the growing Greek-Cypriot community in Camden Town.

Built in 1883, St Dominic's, Southampton Road, is one of the largest Catholic churches in London. The foundation stone was laid by Cardinal Wiseman and despite the card's title, St Dominic's was originally in St Pancras parish. The war memorial inside is by sculptors Eric Gill and Joseph Cribb. The church is now a listed building.

Opened in 1912, St Silas-the-Martyr Church was designed by Ernest Shearman. The procession, probably to mark a first communion, is making its way down Shipton Place towards Prince of Wales Road. The church now stands in a modern housing estate.

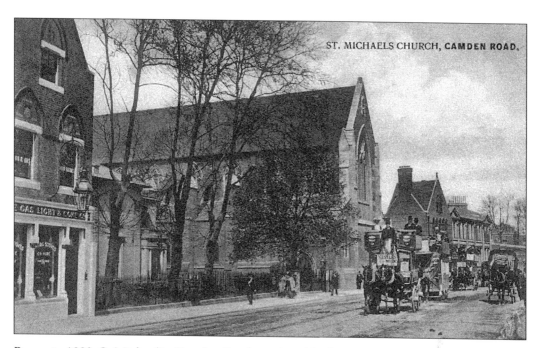

Begun in 1880, St Michael's, Camden Road, is a listed building, overshadowed today by a large Sainsbury's supermarket. Before the church was built, services were held in a nearby shop; to mark the church's 125th anniversary in 2002, the vicar held a service in the same building, which was then being used as a betting shop.

Designed by Charles Hayward and completed in 1866, St Andrew's, Malden Road was demolished in the 1960s as part of wide-scale clearances in the neighbourhood. The façade was of yellow, red and blue brick.

Started in 1882, the Chalk Farm Salvation Army band is one of the oldest and most famous. Much of its early success was down to Alfred W. Punchard (pictured in the oval photograph below). He became Bandmaster in 1894 and remained in the post until 1938. The Salvation Army building on Chalk Farm Road opened in 1923 and was recently rebuilt. The children in the above photograph are posing outside, under a poster advertising a 'thrilling lecture' on China by Commandant and Mrs Cheeseman. As missionary officers they had faced and overcome many obstacles, including Chinese bandits. Officers on home leave would often tour and talk about their work; the Cheesemans' visit probably took place in the late 1920s.

THE CHALK FARM BAND

Four

Dramatic Events

On the evening of 9 June 1857, a fire broke out in the warehouse of Pickfords the carriers, by the Regent's Canal at Camden Town. This picture looks north up Oval Road towards the blaze. Brave volunteers released hundreds of horses stabled in vaults below the warehouse and they stampeded into the surrounding streets. Some were driven towards Highgate and almost overran a startled police inspector on his way to fight the fire. One bad-tempered horse named 'Manhunter' died in the inferno, as he wouldn't allow anyone to lead him out. Large numbers of poultry and goats and upwards of fifty pigs also perished.

Colonel Jack robbing Mrs Smith on the road to Kentish Town, 1734. Late-eighteenth-century newspapers reported: 'robberies and felonious attacks on the Kentish Town road are become very frequent'. The self-named (and possibly fictional) Colonel Jack told the story of how he and his companion Will stole 27s 6d from the two women before running away across the fields to Tottenham Court Road: 'I told them not to scream unless you have mind to force us to murther [murder] you.'

The area near the top of Primrose Hill was a favourite duelling ground during the early nineteenth century as it was then just on the edge of town. Most of the duels were between military men, but in 1809 two employees of Broadwood's, the piano makers, fought over the tuning of a piano! Duels continued to be fought here until the 1830s.

In 1866-67 the Midland Railway line was built across the burial ground of St Pancras Old Church. A national scandal resulted when human remains were found scattered across the site. Thomas Hardy, then a young trainee architect, worked on the project and was appalled at what he saw. In 2002, there were further protests when mechanical diggers damaged coffins while building the Channel Tunnel rail link.

On the evening of 2 September 1861, an excursion train, returning from Kew, hit an empty ballast train on a bridge near Gospel Oak station. A signalman had allowed the passenger train through, without making sure the line was empty. The engine and several carriages left the line, plunging down a steep embankment. At least fourteen people were killed and over 300 injured.

On 2 October 1874, a barge carrying five tons of gunpowder blew up when passing under Macclesfield Bridge on the Regent's Canal. The tremendous explosion killed the crew and destroyed the bridge. Guards at the nearby Regent's Park Barracks were called out, fearing an uprising. Ever since, the rebuilt bridge, which connects Avenue Road to Regent's Park, has been nicknamed 'Blow-up Bridge'.

On 10 June 1886, George Finch shot and killed assistant John Bowes at the Kentish Town sub-post office (No. 165 Brecknock Road). Taking £7 10sh, Finch fled to his home, No. 15 Ospringe Road, where he was discovered hiding in a space above a false ceiling. Finch was an art student, aged nineteen. Indicted for wilful murder, he escaped the death penalty after medical experts testified he was insane.

Daily Mirror

THE MORNING JOURNAL WITH THE SECOND LARGEST NET SALE.

See To-day's 'DAILY MAIL.'

No. 1,286.   Registered at the G.P.O. as a Newspaper.   FRIDAY, DECEMBER 13, 1907.   One Halfpenny.

CAMDEN TOWN MURDER MYSTERY: ROBERT WOOD ON TRIAL FOR HIS LIFE AT THE NEW BAILEY.

In December 1907 the 'Camden Town Murder' of prostitute Emily Dimmock (circular photo) was front-page news. Phyllis, as she was known, was discovered with her throat cut at her home, 29 St Paul's Road. Robert Wood, (top left) a designer at a glassworks in Gray's Inn Road, was charged with her murder. Wood was defended brilliantly by Edward Marshall Hall (picture 4), a leading QC, who later defended Crippen. The Judge's summing up concluded the prosecution had not proved their case, and the jury returned a verdict of 'not guilty'. The case remained unsolved and forgotten until recently, when American crime writer Patricia Cornwell claimed that local artist Walter Sickert was both the Camden Town murderer and Jack the Ripper. Her theory has not been widely accepted.

'Elephants in a Fix'. In March 1884, Sangers Circus was booked to perform at Gospel Oak. Four elephants were transported by rail to Kentish Town but on leaving the trucks, two of the elephants were frightened by engine whistles and bolted. They demolished the station gates and ran up Fortess Road, knocking over a child before finally falling into cellars between Nos 29 and 31 Pemberton Gardens. The other two elephants were then brought up, and by attaching ropes, trainers used them to haul their trapped companions free. All four were then marched off to Gospel Oak, where the circus later played to packed houses.

In 1910, Dr Hawley Harvey Crippen murdered his wife Cora at their home, No. 39 Hilldrop Crescent. Cora had bullied her meek husband and spent well beyond their income, partly to bolster her unsuccessful music hall career as the singer 'Belle Elmore'. Crippen poisoned Cora and buried her in the cellar. With his mistress Ethel le Neve disguised as a young man, Crippen fled to Canada aboard the SS *Montrose* but the suspicious captain alerted the police by wireless, and the couple were arrested before landing. An Old Bailey jury convicted Crippen; he was executed on 23 November 1910. Ethel was acquitted. She later married, had a family and died in 1967. The photograph on the right shows the new owner, music hall artiste Sandy Macnab, a music hall artist, standing at the door of Crippen's house. It has since been demolished, but people report seeing Crippen's ghost nearby.

MRS. PEARCEY.

A MODEL OF THE KITCHEN, containing the identical Furniture and Fixtures from No 2, Priory Street, where Mrs. Hogg and her Baby were murdered.

LIST OF FURNITURE, &c.,

TABLE, CHAIRS, OILCLOTH, COOKING UTENSILS, CROCKERY, FIREPLACE, GRATE, WINDOW AND FLOORING.

THE TABLE against which Mrs. Hogg was supposed to have been leaning when the blows were struck.

THE WINDOW supposed to have been smashed by Mrs. Hogg in her death struggles.

All the articles contained in the Kitchen have been removed from No. 2, Priory Street, and are placed in exact relative position as found by the Police when they entered the premises.

Mrs. PEARCEY'S SITTING ROOM, with her identical Furniture, Couch, Chairs, Table, Mirror, Carpet, Piano, Ornaments, Curtains, Blinds, &c.

The Piano is the one on which Mrs. Pearcey played whilst the Police were searching her house.

Mrs. PEARCEY'S BEDSTEAD and FURNITURE.

THE PERAMBULATOR in which the Bodies were carried.

CASTS OF THE HEADS OF Mrs. HOGG AND HER BABY, taken from Nature after death.

THE CLOTHES worn by Mrs. Hogg and Baby when murdered.

Mrs. PEARCEY'S RECEIPT in her own handwriting.

THE TOFFEE found in the Perambulator.

The Figures of Mr. and Mrs. Hogg and their Baby are placed in the Ground Floor Gallery.

This advert appeared in the 1890-91 Tussaud Catalogue. Mrs Pearcey (real name Mary Wheeler) was a family friend of the Hoggs. But she had been Frank Hogg's mistress before he married Phoebe Styles. On 24 October 1890 Phoebe took her baby to visit Mrs Pearcey at No. 2 Priory (now Ivor) Street, Camden Town. Later, Phoebe's body was discovered in Crossfield Road, off Eton Avenue. Her throat had been cut. The baby's body was found in fields by Finchley Road. When asked to explain the blood on her kitchen walls, Mrs Pearcey repeated over and over again, 'Killing mice.' Despite obvious mental problems, Mrs Pearcey was convicted of the murders and executed. It was Frank who sold the house contents and the pram in which the bodies were transported, to Madame Tussauds, for £200.

Opposite above: This picture was taken after a bombing raid in May 1941. Nellie and her puppies were buried under the kitchen table for five days, at their home in Weedington Road, Kentish Town. By the end of the Second World War, around 19,000 houses in the Borough of St Pancras had been demolished or damaged by bombing, resulting in the deaths of 957 people.

A protest march held in January 1960. St Pancras tenants were fighting a large, means-tested increase in council rents. Over 1,000 refused to pay. Thousands of people marched to the Town Hall and there were violent fights with the police. Despite attracting national press coverage, the campaign failed. Events came to a head in September when bailiffs and police finally evicted the protest leader, who had barricaded himself into his flat in Leighton Road.

This photograph taken in August 1954 shows demonstrators in Grafton Way, off Tottenham Court Road. Cyprus became a British colony in 1925, and groups of Greek-Cypriots first came to live in Camden Town in the 1930s. The community grew steadily and after the invasion of Cyprus by Turkish troops in 1974, more arrived. Enosis was a movement that wanted independence from Britain and union with Greece. Independence was finally granted in 1960.

Five

Industry

This imposing building in Anglers Lane still stands, now modified and hemmed in by houses. Built in 1864 by Claudius Ash & Sons, world-renowned false teeth manufacturers, the kiln with the large chimney was used for firing porcelain teeth. In 1905 the company had a share capital of £1 million pounds. It was later reformed as the Amalgamated Dental Company, who only left in 1965.

Camden and Kentish Towns were a centre of the piano-making industry. Pianos were the main source of Victorian home entertainment. Pictured in 1883, Brinsmead's works in Grafton Road was among the largest. In 1904 the firm produced a piano an hour and at its peak, the factory workforce numbered 300. The firm went out of business in 1920 after a long strike, but the name was bought and 'Brinsmead' pianos continued to be made. Part of the factory buildings still stand in Ryland Road and Perren Street.

The image above dates from the late 1890s and shows the Camden Town empire of wine producers and distillers, W. & A. Gilbey. It was the centre for their gin production and by 1914 the company occupied an amazing twenty acres of floor space! Some was rented from the railway company, notably the Roundhouse (top left), used for storing spirits. The 'Gilbey Special' train departed each day for the docks carrying export goods and during the weeks before Christmas, 4,000-5,000 'two-dozen' cases would be dispatched daily. The packers (below) have been carefully posed to display the firm's name and distinctively shaped gin bottle. The firm left Camden Town in the 1960s.

Camden Brewery bottling stores, 1904. The Camden Brewery on the Regents Canal behind Hawley Crescent was there by 1870. This building on the corner with Kentish Town Road dates from 1900 and is still standing, minus the distinctive adverts for the Brewery's speciality, 'Elephant Pale Ale'. In 1982-83 the site of the main brewery was rebuilt to house TV-AM. MTV Europe are the current occupiers.

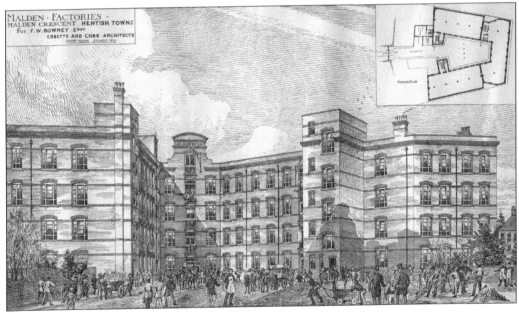

Rowney's large factory was built in Malden Crescent in 1880 at a cost of nearly £20,000. The company began making artists' materials in 1783 and both Constable and Turner used their paints. Currently the company is called Daler-Rowney with a factory in Bracknell. The Malden Crescent factory site has been redeveloped as housing.

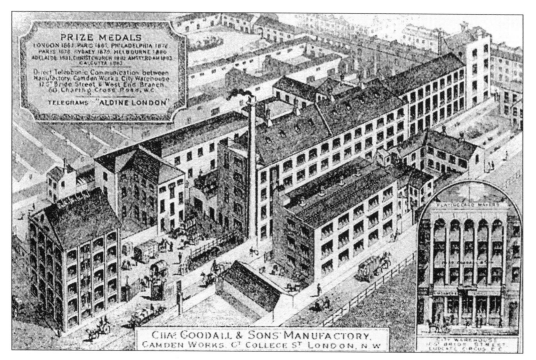

Goodall & Sons' Factory, *c.* 1885. The family firm, which made playing cards, moved to Royal College Street in the 1830s. After duty on a pack of cards was reduced in 1862, the firm expanded and the factory was built. By the early 1900s, their workforce numbered around 1,000 and annual production exceeded 2 million packs of cards. The family sold out to competitors De La Rue in 1922. The factory has since been demolished.

The address of 'The Invalid Patent Bedstead Company' was Anglers Lane. William Jack's invention, patented in 1874, comprised an iron framework that attached to an existing bed. By pulling various levers, the patient could sit up; use the headboard as a table and even position a commode beneath a hole in the mattress!

Carreras' Arcadia Works, Mornington Crescent, 2002. Completed for the cigarette company on the Crescent's communal garden in 1928, it was then the largest concrete building in Britain. The discovery of Tutankhamen's tomb inspired the unusual design. It included two large cats at the entrance, hence the nickname, 'the Black Cat factory'. In 1959 Carreras sold the building, which was converted into offices. In 1999 the exterior was restored to its former glory but the cats are replicas; the original pair was split up, one was moved to a new factory in Basildon and the other sent to Jamaica.

"I prefer Craven "A" — They NEVER Vary!"

CRAVEN "A"

CORK-TIPPED VIRGINIA CIGARETTES

The ONLY Cigarettes Made Specially to Prevent Sore Throats

TWENTY FOR ONE SHILLING   CARRERAS LTD   140 YEARS REPUTATION FOR QUALITY

A 1928 advertisement showing a very chic young woman with her Craven 'A', a popular cigarette made by Carreras. A Spanish nobleman, Don Jose Carreras Ferrer, moved to London in the 1820s, where he sold cigars and founded the company. Named after the Earl of Craven, Craven 'A' cigarettes were launched in 1914 and are still on sale in the UK today.

50

Six

Entertainment

The Zoological Gardens, an engraving by T.H. Shepherd showing Decimus Burton's camel house and clock tower. The zoo opened in Regent's Park in 1828. Admissions rose steeply in 1882 when it was decided to sell Jumbo, an elderly African elephant, to Barnum's Circus. Despite a press campaign to keep him in London, Jumbo was eventually crated up, to be sent by ship to New York. Sadly Jumbo was killed three years later, when he was hit by a train in St Thomas, Ontario. Today London Zoo is renowned for its research and conservation programmes.

A view of St Pancras Wells in 1700, with the old parish church in the background. The spa waters were advertised throughout the eighteenth century for their curative properties, much like those of nearby Hampstead and Kilburn. In 1735, twelve bottles cost 6s. The gardens were laid out with long straight walks shaded by trees, and were used as a promenade by the visitors.

The Assembly House, Kentish Town, c. 1750 (then called the Assembly Rooms). Its attractive two-acre garden drew many visitors with amusements including 'trap-ball'. In this team game, which was as popular as cricket, the batsman released the ball from the 'trap' and, using a stick, hit it as far as possible. In 1725, Robert Wright donated a table to the inn. Allegedly, he had enjoyed a successful convalescence nearby, which included a daily walk to the tavern!

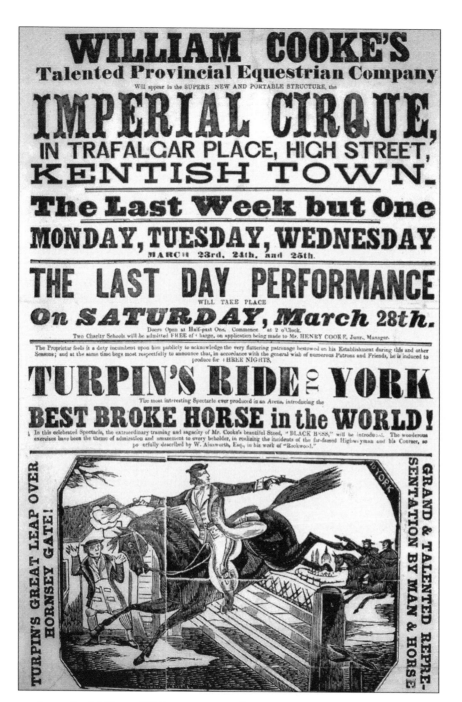

This poster from the 1840s or 1850s invites people to a series of exciting equestrian events at the 'Imperial Cirque', Kentish Town High Street. The entertainment included a reenactment of Dick Turpin's ride to York. William Cooke and his family were well-known equestrian performers who regularly toured the country. Cooke later became manager of Astley's Amphitheatre, near Westminster Bridge, famous for staging historical military dramas. When Dickens put on a private play in 1856 he asked Cooke for advice. The author noted Cooke's arrival 'in an open phaeton drawn by two white ponies with black spots all over them (evidently stencilled)'!

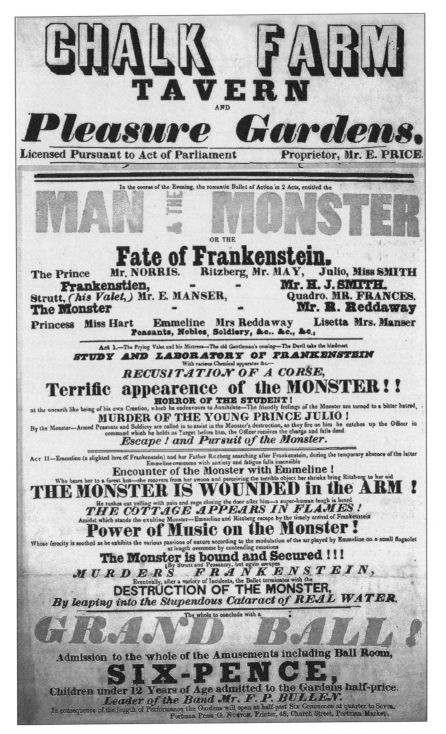

This 1850s poster for *Frankenstein* outlines the exciting events which the audience will see during a 'romantic ballet of action' at the Chalk Farm Tavern, near Primrose Hill. Until the mid-1860s when they were sold for development, the gardens attached to the tavern were well known for their entertainments including foot races, boxing and wrestling matches. There was also a bandstand and dance floor for 1,000 people.

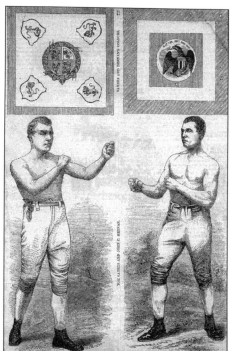

The prize-fighters Tom Sayers (left) and John Heenan (right), 1860. Sayers lived in Bayham Street during the 1840s and '50s, and in Camden Street during the early 1860s. The unconquered champion of England, Sayers fought the American John Heenan at Farnborough in April 1860. Bouts then were unregulated. While Sayers fought one-handed after breaking his right arm, Heenan was cut and couldn't see clearly. The fight was stopped well into its third hour when the crowd invaded the ring, and a draw declared. Sayers retired in May after the public raised £3,000, on condition that he stopped fighting.

In 1865, Sayers died of tuberculosis at a friend's home, No. 257 Camden High Street, now marked by a blue plaque. His funeral attracted a huge crowd and his dog, Lion, was chief mourner. A statue of Lion lies on Sayers' grave in Highgate Cemetery. This image shows the funeral procession leaving Camden Town to drive up Kentish Town and Highgate Roads.

ROYAL
PARK THEATRE

PARK STREET. CAMDEN TOWN.

Proprietress and Manageress ... ... Madame ST. CLAIRE

ENORMOUS SUCCESS !

OF THE

GRAND PANTOMIME,

OF

JACK AND BEANSTALK
THE

By CHARLES MILLWARD, Esq.

EVERYBODY SHOULD SEE
MADAME ROSE BELL

As " JACK,"

MISS KATIE LOGAN

As "ADVENTURE,"

MR. GEORGE TEMPLE

As "THE KING,"

MR. H. M. CLIFFORD

As "THE GIANT."—10 ft. 6 in. high.   The Largest Giant
ever seen on the Stage.

ALSO, THE GORGEOUS
Transformation Scene !

The Versatile BURT as Clown.

MADAME ROSE BELL'S SONGS, "It's Nice," and "The
Nightingale," Encored Five Times Nightly.

MR. GEORGE TEMPLE'S SONGS of "Jack's Yarn," and
"Too Jolly Clever by Half," also Encored Every Evening.

The whole of the Press have pronounced the Royal Park Annual, produced
under the immediate superintendence of Madame St. CLAIRE, to be the best Pantomime this season.

Doors Open at 6.30.   Commence at 7.

The Camden Theatre, *c.* 1904. Opened in 1900 by famous actress Ellen Terry, this Grade II listed building could hold about 2,500 people. Renamed the Hippodrome, 'home to variety', it was soon converted into a cinema. This closed around 1940. The BBC occupied the building from 1945 and a plaque notes the last *Goon Show* was recorded there in April 1972. As the Camden Palace (1982) and Koko (2004), it remains a popular music venue.

Doris Keane, actress and theatre manager, 1921. Born in America, she acted in both London and New York. In 1919 she was Juliet in *Romeo and Juliet* with Ellen Terry, who appeared in her last professional performance as the Nurse. This card advertises Doris' appearance at the Camden Hippodrome, where she starred as an Italian opera singer in *Romance*. She died in 1945 aged sixty-three.

Opposite: This 1878 poster advertises the Christmas pantomime at The Royal Park Theatre, Park Street (today's Parkway). The first theatre on this site was the Alexandra, which became the Royal Park Theatre until it burned down in 1881. It was rebuilt as the Royal Park Hall. A Gaumont cinema opened on the site in 1937 but falling attendance in the 1960s prompted a subdivision into a cinema and bingo hall. Today, after several closures and re-openings, the building offers bingo and a multi-screen complex.

57

Bedford Theatre, Camden High Street, 1904. First opened in 1861 as a music hall in the garden of the Bedford Arms, re-building in the late 1890s transformed the Bedford into one of London's premier music halls. Famous artistes such as Marie Lloyd, Gracie Fields and Charlie Chaplin played there, while Belle Elmore, Crippen's unfortunate wife, also appeared. The interior was recorded by the paintings of Walter Sickert. Between 1933 and 1939 it became an ABC cinema before reverting to a theatre which finally closed in 1951. Demolition and redevelopment followed in 1968.

Artist Walter Sickert with his third wife, Therese, photographed in 1940, two years before his death. Sickert painted scenes from the music halls, including the Bedford, and he led the Camden Town group of artists. He lived at several addresses in the area: No. 6 Mornington Crescent (1905-1911), No. 68 Gloucester Crescent (1912-1915), and No. 81 Camden Road (1917-1920).

In 1907, a local shop displayed an advert for 'H. Bale, Thursday December 5th, Prince of Wales Public Baths and Hall, Plain and Fancy Dress Ball'. Some of the costumes are extremely elaborate and, for the most part, impossible to 'decode' but the lady in the patchwork dress carries the sign 'Miss Lino.'

The Plaza, No. 211 Camden High Street, 1982. Now redeveloped, it opened as the Electric Theatre in 1909, becoming the Theatre DeLuxe (1914), then the Britannia Picture Palace (1919), and lastly, the Plaza in 1938. From 1977 it specialised in foreign films, closing in 1994. *The Wishing Tree* by Russian director Tengiz Abuladze, concerned a community on the eve of the Russian Revolution.

Opposite below: The Forum, Highgate Road, 2003. Opened in 1934 as the Forum Theatre, the Forum was in fact a cinema, seating 2,175. It was taken over by the ABC chain a year later and closed in 1970. Reborn as the 'Town and Country Club' it became a popular live music venue in the 1980s, and remains so, under its original name.

The 1934-35 programme for the Forum. Films were not the only attraction. Audiences would be entertained by performances on the Compton organ, which rose majestically from the floor. Patrons could also visit the lounge and dance hall on the first floor, where daily tea and supper dances were held.

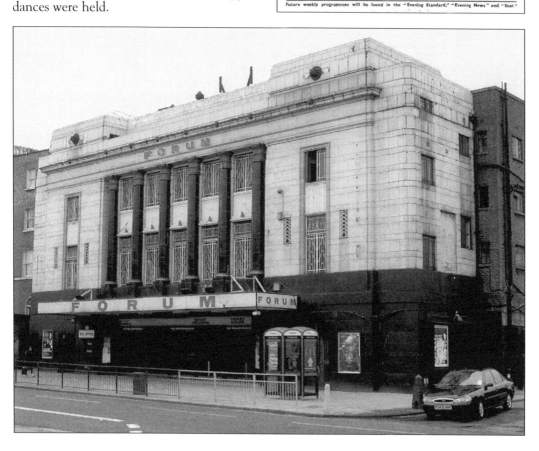

This acrobatic display took place at the public baths, Prince of Wales Road, probably when the building opened in 1901. Unfortunately, there are no details of who is performing.

Parliament Hill Fields Lido, soon after it was opened in 1937-38. Now a listed building, it was one of thirteen open-air pools built by the LCC and is considered an outstanding example of the genre. The fountains at each end of the pool acted as water aerators and clearly proved popular with younger swimmers. The Lido was refurbished in 2005.

Children swinging on a lamp post, photographed somewhere in 1960s Kentish Town. This was a popular street game that made use of the old style, lower lamp posts which had a convenient bar to attach the rope, just below the glass lantern.

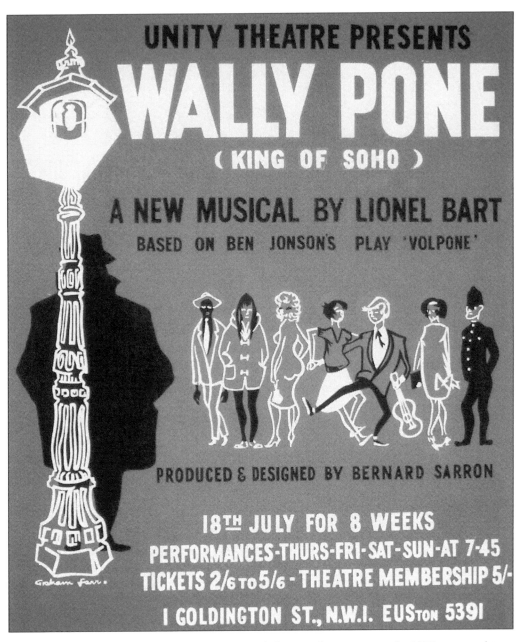

UNITY THEATRE PRESENTS

WALLY PONE
(KING OF SOHO)

A NEW MUSICAL BY LIONEL BART
BASED ON BEN JONSON'S PLAY 'VOLPONE'

PRODUCED & DESIGNED BY BERNARD SARRON

18TH JULY FOR 8 WEEKS
PERFORMANCES-THURS-FRI-SAT-SUN-AT 7·45
TICKETS 2/6 TO 5/6 - THEATRE MEMBERSHIP 5/-
1 GOLDINGTON ST., N.W.I. EUSTON 5391

Graham Farr.

The Unity Theatre playbill, 1958. Unity was a left-wing theatre group. In 1937 it moved into a disused Methodist chapel in Goldington Street, subsequently converted into a 320-seat theatre. Among the many distinguished actors associated with Unity were Alfie Bass, Michael Gambon, Bill Owen and Paul Robeson. In 1962 Unity reported that of 179 productions staged, 106 were new scripts and thirty-five were world premieres of foreign plays; for example, the first Bertolt Brecht play seen in the UK. *Wally Pone* was by Lionel Bart, an original musical satire on the coffee bar culture of the 1950s. In 1975 the theatre was badly damaged by fire and never really recovered. The site was bought by the St Pancras Housing Association in 1988 and redeveloped.

Seven

Civic Pride

Mealtime, St Pancras Workhouse, St Pancras Way, c. 1901. This was the last of several different workhouse sites. The workhouse was central to housing and 'helping' the poor. They were unpleasant places – inmates worked hard for no wages, couples were separated and family contact kept to a minimum. St Pancras regularly sent pauper children as young as eight to work in the cotton mills. They received no wages and, if they survived, could only leave when they reached twenty-one. In 1851, forty pauper children were sent to Bermuda. Despite reports of their being very happy, many said the children were being used as slave labour.

The Tailors' Benevolent Institution opened in 1842 at the corner of Prince of Wales Road and Queen's Crescent. A home for 'aged tailors', each pensioner received £20 a year plus coals and candles. A local resident recalled, 'the church bell would toll for a death and we would keep our heads under the bed clothes in case a ghost appeared'. In 1939 a block of council flats replaced the Institution.

St Pancras Almshouses, Southampton Road, c. 1900. This charitable foundation for aged pensioners was established in 1850. Now Grade II listed, the thirteen almshouses opened in 1860, after the original buildings in Wilkin Street were swept away by the Hampstead Junction Railway. In 1881 there were sixty elderly inmates. Renamed Fraser Regnart Court, they still provide sheltered housing.

The free treatment of animals – the 'cheap practice' – in 1891, at the Royal Veterinary College. Opened in 1791 in Great College Street (later renamed Royal College Street), the college took a leading role in establishing veterinary science in England. Originally horses and donkeys - the main means of transport - made up a high percentage of all patients. Royal patronage was confirmed by charter in 1875. The site had stabling, a Turkish bath for horses, a pharmacy, forge, operating theatre, dissecting room and a museum of specimens. Rebuilt in 1937 and part of London University since 1949, the college now has a second campus in Potters Bar, and treats more than 17,000 animals annually.

Orphan Working School, Maitland Park. — Haverstock Hill.

In 1847, another of the neighbourhood's large institutions, the Alexandra Orphan Working School, moved from east London to its new building near Haverstock Hill. It housed about 500 children; the boys left to become apprentices while the girls entered domestic service. A teacher requested a friend not to communicate by postcard 'as everyone reads them'. Flats have replaced the orphanage. Two of the smaller buildimgs survived until recently, but all that now remains are the gateposts (minus lamps).

Prince of Wales Road & St. Pancras Baths Kentish Town N. W.

This display of schoolwork is taking place at the St Pancras Public Baths, in the Willis Pool, possibly soon after the baths opened. During the winter months at least one of the swimming baths was temporarily converted into a hall. Most of the local schools had contributed to the display.

Opposite: The St Pancras Public Baths, Prince of Wales Road, opened in October 1901, when the Building Superintendent took 'the First Plunge'. Many homes lacked proper washing facilities, so, in addition to four swimming pools, this building also provided personal 'slipper' baths, plus fifty sinks with mangles, irons and a drying room. Originally there were separate entrances for Men's 1st and 2nd Class (baths), Ladies (baths), Public Hall and Public Washhouse, still visible today. The facility has recently been completely refurbished.

St Pancras Town Hall (building on left), St Pancras Way. The first Town Hall on the site opened in 1847, but this frontage dates from 1874-75. Designed to accommodate thirty staff, by 1924 numbers had risen to 110, with eighteen clerks in one room alone! In 1937 a new Town Hall on Euston Road was opened and is currently used by the Borough of Camden.

Looking south down Pancras Road, past the gardens of Goldington Square, c. 1905. You can just see the edge of the town hall on the left, with the substantial block of the St Pancras Workhouse extension beyond, by the same architect as the town hall. Opened in 1885 as an infirmary, it now forms part of St Pancras Hospital.

The opening ceremony of Goldington Buildings (now Goldington Court) in Crowndale Road, 4 June 1904. Officiating in the front row is Mayor Thomas Idris, who owned a mineral water factory just round the corner. This was the first block of municipal flats built by St Pancras Council; the weekly rent was 3s 6d for one room. An early resident was Ethel le Neve, Crippen's mistress.

Arlington (originally Rowton) House, Arlington Road, 1984. The philanthropist Lord Rowton wanted to provide single male workers with decent housing, 'fit for an archbishop'. Opened in 1905 with 985 cubicles and 118 small bedrooms, this was the largest of the six Rowton Houses in London. Renovated and remodelled in 2010, it continues to provide accommodation for homeless people.

This ornate fountain is on Gloucester Gate Bridge, rebuilt in 1877-78. The fountain was donated by Mrs Kent, wife of the churchwarden. The female figure by Joseph Durham ARA is called 'Early Morn'. She still stands on Cornish boulders, shielding her eyes from the sun. Sadly, the water, which once gushed into the bucket below her feet no longer flows. HRH Duke of Cambridge performed the opening ceremony of the bridge, followed by a marquee lunch with musical interludes and speeches, held in the nearby zoo.

Opposite: St Pancras mobile library during the Second World War. This library was well attended by ARP wardens; dogs were barred, but clearly pipe smoking was not! The board outside carries the quote: 'Books offer the human intellect the means whereby civilisation may be carried triumphantly forward'.

The subjects chosen for the statues on the new Gloucester Gate Bridge reflected the neighbourhood: Regent's Park, its canal and playing fields as well as the nearby barracks. Made using clay quarried from the bridge foundations, pictured here is a group of athletes; the other groups comprised soldiers, fisher and flower maidens. Unfortunately the terracotta deteriorated and the statues were removed.

Unveiling the Cobden statue, 27 June 1868, near Mornington Crescent. The statue, of Sicilian marble, is by W. & T. Wills of Euston Road. Richard Cobden MP was best known for his campaign to abolish the Corn Laws. Unfortunately, it proved hard to raise money for the statue and the final few pounds were still owed on the morning of the unveiling! Napoleon III was a major contributor as Cobden had negotiated a free trade treaty with France. Cobden's widow Catherine was present at the ceremony; the boys of the North London Collegiate School were also watching from the windows of the building on the right (later Oetzmann's factory).

Eight

Education

This picture shows a tailoring class at the boys' home for the 'training and maintenance of destitute boys not convicted of crime'. Originally opened on Euston Road in 1858, the extension of the Midland Railway necessitated a move in 1865 to Nos 115-117 Regent's Park Road. Every boy was carefully vetted. In one instance, a navy chaplain secured a place for a fourteen-year-old who had stowed away and sailed round the world to China and Hong Kong, returning to the UK ill and destitute. Despite this, on leaving the home, he promptly decided to become a sailor!

A dame school somewhere in Camden Town, with children learning the alphabet. These small private schools were usually run by an elderly woman, hence their name. She taught working-class children to read and write, as well as useful skills such as sewing. Weekly fees were about 3d, but the quality of education that the children received varied enormously.

SOUTHAMPTON HOUSE ACADEMY, KENTISH TOWN, MIDDLESEX.

CONDUCTED BY

Rev.d John Bickerdike

Southampton House Academy, now 137 Highgate Road. In 1828 this private school for boys was charging annual fees of 24 guineas. Reverend John Bickerdike was the headmaster until 1849. The main building still stands north of the railway bridge and has been renovated, but the playground was lost when the railway was built in the 1860s.

Gospel Oak Schools, Allcroft Road, 1867. There were classrooms for 700-800 boys, girls and infants. Renamed 'William Ellis School' in 1889 after its founder, it then became a boys' secondary school, and moved to a new building on Highgate Road in 1937. The two left-hand buildings with peaked roofs remain, altered and now used as a community hall. Writer Len Deighton attended William Ellis.

The North London School of Drawing and Modelling, 1852. Opened in 1850, this evening school offered classes for both sexes but aimed primarily at improving working men's skills. The artist Ford Maddox Brown was on the managing committee. Here, three groups are being tutored in a large room attached to the Bedford Arms Tavern off Camden High Street. The Bedford Music Hall had taken over the space by 1861.

The Governesses Institution, Prince of Wales Road, opened in June 1849. Residents had to be over sixty with an annual income under £20. Funding problems and 'shrill shrieks' from the nearby railway prompted a move to Chislehurst in 1872. Four schools successively occupied the building, the last one, Sir Richard of Chichester, closing in 1999. Grade II listed, the building is being redeveloped as flats.

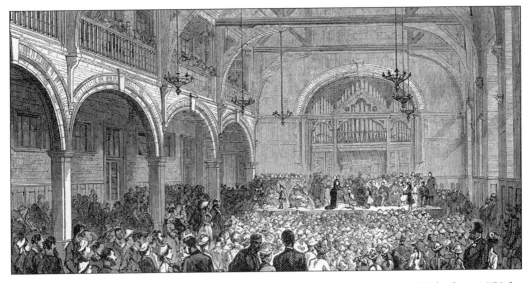

Prize-giving, North London Collegiate School, Sandall Road, 1879. Established in 1850 by Frances Mary Buss, pioneer in women's education, the school moved here in 1879. In July, crowds welcomed the Prince and Princess of Wales, who came to distribute prizes. The girls moved out of London in 1939, which was fortunate, as subsequent bombing badly damaged the building. After the Second World War, Camden School for Girls (another Buss foundation) moved into the rebuilt premises.

VIEW OF THE CAMDEN TOWN INFANT & SUNDAY SCHOOLS.

Camden Town Infant and Sunday School and adjoining master's house, 1836, designed by T.M. Nelson. In 1834, the National Society approached the Treasury for a grant of £200 to help establish the school in Camden Street, next to All Saints church. But it was decided to award just £100 towards the estimated £341 building costs. This later became the Camden Town National School.

Camden Town National School, class 4, early 1900s. National Schools for the Education of the Poor preceded Board Schools, which were established after 1870. The rules stated pupils must have 'clean faces, ears and hands, their hair properly cut and combed and their clothes neatly mended and clean'.

The Boys' Home, Regent's Park Road, N.W.

By 1890, there were more than 150 boys at the boys' home, Regent's Park Road. As well as learning a trade, they raised funds by delivering firewood or cleaning knives and shoes. Lessons included the basic three 'R's plus some history, geography, drawing and singing. Over 1,000 boys were trained during the home's sixty-year life. Closed in 1920, much of the building survives.

Drill at the boys' home was at 6.15 a.m. each morning. There was an excellent band. It led the boys each Wednesday to play football on Primrose Hill, and was hired out for garden parties and events at the Zoo. Many used this experience to enlist in the army as band boys.

Kentish Town Church of England School, Islip Street, 'Group 4', 1913. This postcard was sent to a relative in New Zealand. The school was built in 1849 as the Kentish Town National, and part of the building survives as a school today.

Rhyl Street School, Kentish Town, was a London Board School opened in 1898. It shows the

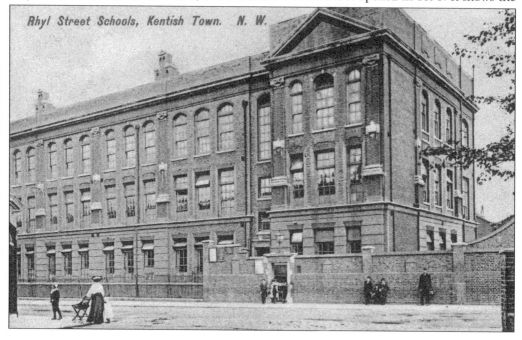

typical 'triple decker' design, usually with boys on the top floor, girls on the first and infants on the ground floor. A group of pupils stands in front of the 'Boys' entrance, which is still in place today, as are the original railings.

The County Secondary School for girls (now Parliament Hill School), Highgate Road, opened in September 1914. It replaced the original school established in 1906 in nearby Ingestre Road. A pupil recalled visiting the Highgate Road site on 'botany trots' before the new school was built. Then occupied by a derelict house in overgrown grounds, 'we were forbidden to attempt to get in, as [the house] was considered too dangerous'.

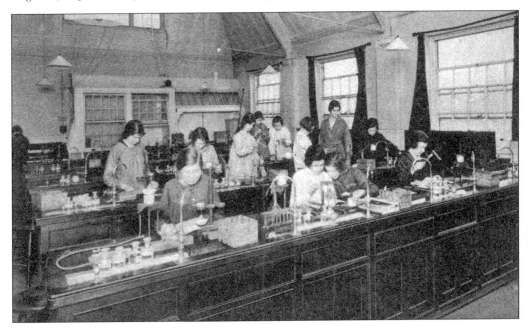

The chemistry laboratory, County Secondary School, before the Second World War. In 1956 Dame Edith Evans opened a range of new school buildings. The 425 pupils were then joined by a further 390 girls transferring from local schools. The planned roll was 1,350.

North Western Polytechnic, 1993. Designed by W.E. Riley, the polytechnic opened at the junction of Prince of Wales and Kentish Town Roads in 1929. Absorbed into the Polytechnic of North London, it later became part of the University of North London, which shut the Kentish Town building in 1996. It has been sympathetically redeveloped as flats and a restaurant but the owners are seeking to demolish part of the site.

Working Men's College, Crowndale Road, soon after opening in 1906. The date of 1854 refers to the original foundation in Red Lion Square, established by F.D. Maurice, Charles Kingsley, and other members of the Christian Socialists. As an adult education college, today it caters for over 9,000 students, both men and women.

Acland School, Fortess Road. Another tall London Board School opened in 1898, it was demolished when the new Acland Burghley School was built nearby, in Burghley Road. The Fortess Road site is now occupied by the modern, low-rise Eleanor Palmer Primary School.

Holmes Road Institute, 2002. Opened in 1874 as a Board School for over 1,000 children, it was later enlarged to take another 500. Declining numbers meant that by 1931 the building was converted to adult education. To raise local morale during the Second World War, popular comedians Flanagan and Allen performed their theme song, 'Underneath the Arches', beneath the arches of the covered playground. Today, the building is still used for adult education by Westminster Kingsway College.

The forty-one children of Class 5, Torriano Avenue School, in the 1960s. Another Board School – Conan Doyle recognized their educational aspirations by having Sherlock Holmes call them 'beacons of the future' – it opened in 1910. Pupils who attended the 'British School' in Kentish Town Road (later No. 158) moved to Torriano Road when the school opened.

Holy Rood Convent, Gloucester Avenue, c. 1904. The Catholic order of the 'Helpers of the Holy Souls' moved into Park House in 1882 and later rebuilt it as Holy Rood House. The site has recently been developed as private housing. The ornate lamp illuminated the York & Albany public house on the corner of Park Village East.

EDUCATION OF YOUTH.

A GENTLEMAN of Respectability, assissted by able and well selected Masters, has opened a SEMINARY for the Reception of YOUNG GENTLEMEN, from Three to Ten Years of Age, in a very airy Situation, the CORNER of CAMDEN-STREET, near PANCRAS CHURCH.

The Plan of Education comprises a thorough instruction in the ENGLISH LANGUAGE, its Grammar, and a distinct and clear Manner of reading.—FRENCH in its purity, and the RUDIMENTS of LATIN, according to the most approved Forms of the great English Schools.

Religion and Morals are the first Objects in view. Care will be directed also to other points, of the utmost Importance to Children of the tender Age included in this Plan—Health, Comfort, and Cleanliness: He engages to promote this, by unremitted Attention to wholesome and plentiful Provision, moderate and healthful Exercise, Beds and Rooms clean, airy, and not crowded.

Considering that at a tender age, Restraint and Severity can only produce Unhappiness, without forwarding real Improvement, the Pupils are led by gentle Means to the love of Science and Virtue; so as to present them, at a proper period, eminently qualified to take an advanced Station in a public School, or to be speedily accomplished for such professional or other Pursuits, as are to engage the ensuing Portion of their Lives.

TERMS.					ENTRANCE.		
Board and Tuition -	£26	5	0	a Year.	£2	2	0
French - - - -		1	1	0		1	1	0
Writing and Arithmetic	0	15	0			0	10	6
Latin - - - - -		1	1	0	per Quarter.	1	1	0
Dancing - - - -		1	1	0		1	1	0
Military Exercise -	0	15	0			0	10	6
Sleeping alone - -		1	1	0			
Assistants and Servants	1	1	0	a Year.			
Any Pupil remaining during the Vacations, to pay	2	2	0	each Vacation.			

Each Pupil to bring Half a Dozen Towels, a Table Spoon, and a White handled Knife and Fork.

C. Stower, Printer, Charles Street, Hatton Garden.

An 1803 prospectus for a private school in Camden Street, near St Pancras Old Church. It shows the fees and the type of education the young gentlemen would receive. There were many such establishments in London at the time. Note the instruction at the end to bring their own towels and cutlery.

Nine

Camden Town Traders

Frederick Greenwood at work in the 1950s at Edward Gerrard & Sons, taxidermists, No. 61 College Place. Edward Gerrard, naturalist and friend of Charles Darwin, started the business in Camden Town in 1853. Then, customers often returned with 'big game' trophies but when interviewed in 1954 the fourth generation owner commented ruefully, 'very little big stuff these days'. The shop featured in Alfred Hitchcock's 1956 film *The Man Who Knew Too Much* starring James Stewart and Doris Day. The scene includes a bizarre confrontation between Stewart and a man wielding a swordfish! In 1979, now trading from Royal College Street, Gerrard's weekly hire charge for a stuffed bison was £75.

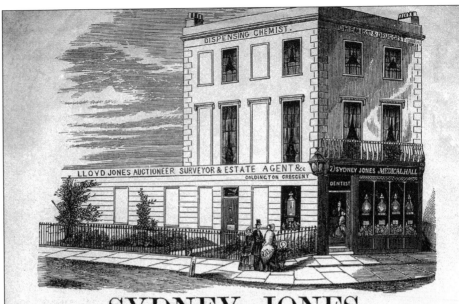

An early advertisement for Sidney Jones' chemist's shop in Crowndale Road (where Crowndale Court now stands). Doubling as a dentist, Jones stocked cosmetics, spices and groceries as well as selling leeches and medicines. A local resident recalled being given a yellowish lump of foul-tasting 'Turkish Rhubarb' to nibble for toothache. His cough was treated by Ipecacuanha wine and syrup of squills.

Parkes Drug Stores, No. 173 Camden High Street, near the Parkway junction. This advertising card was posted to a local resident in 1909. There were other branches in London; all promised to collect orders and promptly deliver prescription and any other chemist goods to your door. A dentist operated from upstairs, charging 21s for a set of dentures. The shop is still a chemist, with a modern frontage.

THE PRESS, at 88, Camden Road, 1862.

Printed by PREMO PRESS,
(formerly Warren Hall & Lovitt, Established 1852),
211, GREAT COLLEGE STREET, LONDON, N.W. 1
(Printers to St Thomas', Agar Town, since 1863),

An advertisement for a Camden Town printers, the Premo Press, based in Great (later Royal) College Street. Their Caxton print works were nearby, at No. 88 Camden Road. It shows the press (established by their predecessors Warren Hall and Lovitt) as it appeared in 1862.

Park Street (later Parkway), looking south, *c.* 1924. The first premises on the left, numbers 110-112, rebuilt in 1904, were occupied by Benjamin Barling & Sons (as recorded by carved initials over the door). Barlings were famous pipe-makers who started as jewellers in Soho. The firm moved to 142 Camden High Street in around 1841, and by 1884 they were at Park Street where they continued to trade until 1970.

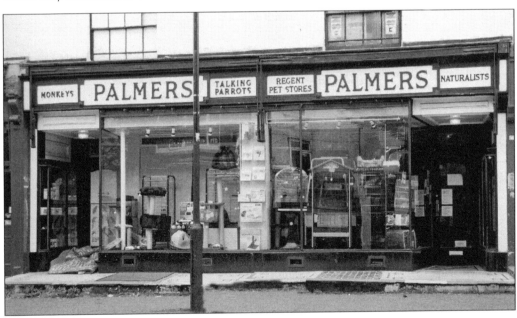

Palmers pet shop, Parkway, 2002. Opened in 1918, Palmers provided the model for the 'zoological shop' in Graham Greene's story *It's a Battlefield* (1934). Twenty years later, a chimpanzee escaped from his cage and set free parrots, baby alligators, two gibbons and a python. For a while in 1969, the owner intentionally allowed a boa constrictor to roam free at night, to deter burglars! The shop moved across the road in 2005, but the original sign remains above a restaurant.

Wellington Street, (now Inverness Street), before the First World War, with Teetgen, tea merchants, on the corner with the High Street. House building here began at the time of Waterloo, which probably explains the original name. This has long been a market street; stallholders would stay open late into Saturday evening and sell off any remaining goods at knockdown prices.

Inverness Street, 1950s, showing the busy market, which still flourishes, though the shops have been 'gentrified'. In the 1960s, Reggie's junk stall was a fruitful source of 'bargains', from books and clothes, to household and electrical goods. One stall displayed a rubbery, processed pink animal food in a big block, which was cut and sold by weight.

The business was started by Edwin Trill, in Brighton. In the 1890s his brother Harold took over a stationer's shop at No. 131 Camden High Street, moving to No. 123 by 1913. The business crossed the road to No. 78 in 1940, and continued trading there until the mid-1980s. The black cats are surely an allusion to the statues outside the nearby Carreras Factory. Both Harold and his son were elected Mayor of St Pancras.

Percival Noah Brazil's pork butchers shop at No. 178 Camden High Street, c. 1906. The site was rebuilt after WWII. Kentish Town customers could shop at the firm's Queens Crescent branch. An open-air display of meat was the norm, and problems during the summer heat gave rise to the saying, 'never buy pork unless there's an 'r' in the month'.

Looking north up Camden High Street, from the junction with Pratt Street, *c.* 1904. The mast was used by the newly-opened National Telephone Company at No. 106. In the background, the shop awnings and flag mark the site of the extensive premises of Bowman Brothers, Camden Town's leading store.

In 1864, brothers Thomas and Robert Bowman opened an upholstery business in Camden Town. The firm rapidly expanded to occupy Nos 112-138 Camden High Street, offering an extensive range of furniture and household goods. Pictured here in around 1904, the cluttered display of china was typical of the time. The business closed in the 1980s.

In April 1903, the boot makers at No. 135 Camden High Street were advertising a 'Special Sale'. In addition to flour, corn and seeds, the shop next door sold Spratt's animal food. Spratt started by selling lightning conductors but went on to patent dog biscuits called 'Spratt's Meat Fibrine Dog Cake'. Spratt's young assistant Charles Cruft established the famous dog show.

Camden High Street, *c.* 1904. Teetgen's delivery cart, loaded with Huntley & Palmer biscuit boxes, stands outside their shop at the corner with Inverness Street. The buildings on the right, north of the tube station, have all been demolished and an open-air market established on their site. The Bucks Head pub still stands at the corner of Buck Street, minus its corner pub sign.

MORITZ BEHR,

(Late GRIMSTER,)

Wholesale & Retail Tobacco

& CIGAR DEALER,

8, Delancy St., Camden Town.

Licensed Victuallers & the Trade Supplied.

Pipes Cleaned, Mounted, & Repaired.

Advertising cards such as these were given away by many Victorian businesses. As early as 1863, Grimster had a tobacconist shop in Warren Street, Camden Town, and was still there four years later, when the road was renamed Delancey Street. His successor, Moritz Behr, had left by 1874, when a Mr Banham had the shop.

Oetzmann's cabinet factory, 1904, on Camden High Street, opposite the Cobden statue. In 1848, company founder John Oetzmann opened his first shop at No. 67 Hampstead Road, dealing in china and glass. The company diversified to offer a full range of household furniture and goods from their nine showrooms in Hampstead Road and a shop in Tottenham Court Road. The factory closed in 1957 and the site was redeveloped.

Nos 218-224 Camden High Street, 2002. The Elephant's Head pub (top left) recalls the Elephant pale ale once produced by the Camden Brewery, just around the corner. Today the High Street is known for its large, colourful 3-D advertising signs.

Camden Lock Place, Camden Lock, 2002. Camden Lock Market and the surrounding streets have become a major tourist attraction, drawing millions of visitors every year. The Grade II listed Interchange Warehouse in the background is now occupied by offices.

Joseph Jupp's butcher's shop, No. 158 Regents Park Road, 1910. Judging by the number of delivery carts, this was a substantial business. The sender of the postcard asked it be given 'to Ernie', possibly the young man marked with an 'x' in the photograph.

Despite Jupp's being just a few minutes walk away, Primrose Hill residents could also buy their meat from Turners, on the corner of Fitzroy Road and St George's (now Chalcot) Road. In 1905, the sender of this postcard was lodging with the assistant in the white apron. Today the shop sells pottery.

Ten

Time Gentlemen Please!

Bull and Gate, 389 Kentish Town Road, 1904. It seems unlikely, but one source says the name was a corruption of 'Boulogne Gate'. This was one of eleven pubs existing in Kentish Town in 1721. This 'splendid modern gin-palace' was completed in 1871; the large ornamental lamps were probably added in the 1890s. Today the pub provides a major venue for a wide range of bands.

Assembly House, 1849. According to the *Illustrated London News*, 'A terrific storm was very severely felt in Kentish-town. Here the lightning struck a remarkably fine old elm. Some of the larger limbs nearly fell on a man who was passing.' Rebuilt in 1853, the present building by Kentish Town architects Thorpe and Furniss dates from the late 1890s. Grade II listed, the interior still retains some of the Victorian woodwork and etched glass.

The Castle Inn, 1800, another very old pub. Its tea gardens bordered the Fleet river where an anchor was found in the eighteenth century, indicating the stream was possibly once navigable to this point. Rebuilt in 1848-49, a tile panel showing jousting knights by a castle wall was added later. Now (2011) a local music venue, the building has been painted black and renamed 'Heroes'.

Brecknock Arms, Camden Road, a card postmarked 1905. This was the scene in 1843 of a duel (allegedly the last fought in London). Lieutenant Munro shot his brother-in-law, Colonel Fawcett, who died two days later. After escaping abroad, Munro returned to face trial. He was convicted of murder, but his sentence was commuted to a year's imprisonment. The building is now called The Unicorn.

The Tally Ho! pub, Fortess Road, 1904, with its wonderfully elaborate lamps. The fashion for these lights dates from the 1880s and 1890s, when many pubs were rebuilt or refurbished. In 1899 the fixing of bracket lamps that projected more than a limited distance was forbidden by the LCC, but seemingly, few publicans complied and removed existing fixtures. The pub has recently been demolished.

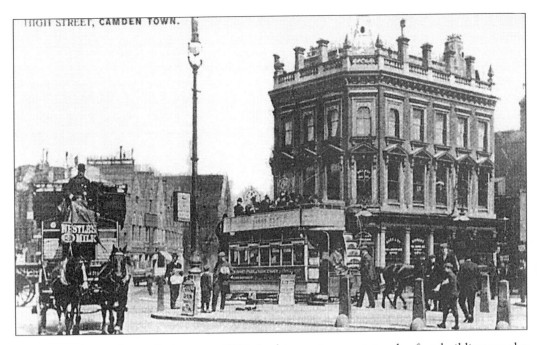

Mother Red Cap, facing Parkway, *c.* 1910. Its history is uncertain: the first building on the site possibly dates from the late seventeenth century, while its early names may have included Halfway House or Mother Damnable's. Today's pub lacks the decorative roof pillars and balustrade. The name was changed yet again to The World's End in 1986 and it currently has a popular music venue downstairs.

The Dublin Castle in Parkway, 2002. This is one of the pubs that make Camden Town well known for live music. Numerous bands have played here, including Madness, who started here as a local band in the late 1970s.

The Queens, Regents Park Road, opened in the 1850s. The statue of Shakespeare was recently removed but the names of past amusements are still visible on the first-floor window glass, including 'pyramids', a form of billiards. The actor Sir Robert Stevens and writer Kingsley Amis are numbered among famous faces seen drinking here. The motor bus was built in 1905, with bodywork by Birch of Kentish Town.

The Adelaide opposite Chalk Farm tube station, 1906, looking west along Adelaide Road. Named after Queen Adelaide, wife of William IV, the pub was built in the 1840s. Until recently, the area in front was a bus terminus. *The Geisha*, advertised on the bus, was playing at Dalys in 1906. Following a rebuild after a fire in 1985, the pub was replaced by commercial premises.

Chalk Farm Tavern, in the 1840s. Chalk House Farm, a small alehouse, appears in the licensing records from at least 1732. After 1790, the new landlord Thomas Rutherford heavily promoted his 'Chalk Farm Tavern and Tea Gardens', offering good food, drink and entertainment. During the 1830s, inquests were held in the Tavern's Long Room on the deaths of navvies who had been killed by earth falls while building the nearby London to Birmingham Railway. Today's building in Regent's Park Road on the corner with Erskine Road dates from 1854, and is currently a restaurant.

Eleven

Kentish Town Traders

Rayner's Pork butchers, No. 74 Queens Crescent, *c*. 1926. Over the years, this busy shopping street has seen more than thirty butchers trading from various sites, as well as from market stalls. This elaborate window display was in one of Rayner's three shops in Queens Crescent. The seven pigs have been arranged to look as if they are happily foraging for food.

Beddall's, Nos 293-299 Kentish Town Road, on the corner with Holmes Road, pictured soon after rebuilding in 1900. Owned by Herbert Beddall, it was one of the largest drapery businesses in the neighbourhood, also briefly trading from Nos 303-305. The site has since been redeveloped as shops with office space above.

C. & A. Daniels, 207-211a Kentish Town Road, December 1903. In 1865 Charles and Alfred Daniels started their drapers business in a single shop. By 1913/14, the firm had expanded to occupy ten of the shops between Prince of Wales Road and Anglers Lane. The parents of author V.S. Pritchett met at the store in the 1890s; he was a shopwalker, she a milliner: 'She could put an ugly hat on a grumbling woman, give a twist, snatch a feather or a bunch of cherries and so dazzle the customer with chatter and her smiles.' The male employees 'lived over the shop', where working hours were 8 a.m. to 8 p.m. on weekdays and 8 a.m. to 11 p.m. on Saturday! It remained a family business until sold in 1954, finally closing in the mid-1960s.

Opposite: Kentish Town Road, looking south from the junction with Patshull Road (left), *c.* 1905. The rows of globe lamps on the right mark the premises of Kentish Town's leading department store, C. & A. Daniels, who also traded from No. 178 opposite. A few doors down at No. 172, was another branch of Brazil's the butcher.

George Arnold, jeweller and pawnbroker, Nos 213-215 Kentish Town Road, 1903. Arnold had been in the trade for around seventy years. Moving from Shoreditch, he bought an existing pawnbroker's business in Kentish Town in the mid-1870s. Just after the Second World War, the UK had over 5,000 pawnbrokers; it was possible to serve 1,000 customers on a busy Friday or Saturday.

Blustons, Nos 213-215 Kentish Town Road, 2003. The ladies outfitters moved in when the pawnbrokers (shown above) closed in the late 1920s. Amazingly, just two firms have occupied this double shop since the 1870s! Blustons was started by the present owner's grandparents. At its peak, the business had eight shops, one at 70 Oxford Street, all managed by family members.

James Barley, undertaker, May 1904. The elaborate lamp illuminated the corner of No. 97 Kentish Town Road with Clarence Road. The window display shows Barley could provide 'funeral hatchments', a painted coat of arms in a diamond-shaped lozenge. After the funeral procession, this was fixed to the deceased's house for a year before being deposited in the church. The 1901 census has James Barley living above the shop, with his wife and twelve children; the youngest, Horace, is probably pictured here. The modified building still stands, now on the corner of a cul-de-sac.

In 1903, Salmon and Gluckstein, No. 197 Kentish Town Road, correctly claimed to be the 'largest tobacconists in the world', with 140 shops. But this was not their only business – family members were co-founders of J. Lyons & Co., which opened teashops up and down the country. They also built the Trocadero in London's West End. At its peak, Lyons was Europe's largest food producer.

Henry John Sibley ran the Grafton Studios at No. 181 Kentish Town Road, from at least 1885 to 1908. A second branch in the Euston Road had opened by 1890. With so much competition, photographers began to use more and more elaborate decorations on the backs of their portrait cards. In 1901 Sibley was living over the shop; his son Francis worked as his assistant.

Martin Birdseye, No. 310 Kentish Town Road, 1902. Birdseye supplemented sales of corn and animal food by doing removals and hiring out horses or vans. 'Canary guano' was also for sale, plus three grades of flour with an ascending price scale according to purity: 'Households', 'Kentish Whites' and 'Lily'. Birdseye Frozen Foods were not established in New York until 1922, so it's unlikely Martin was connected.

J. Sainsbury, Nos 250-254 Kentish Town Road, 1955. This was one of three Sainsbury stores on Kentish Town Road, all now closed. The wraparound glass frontage gave shoppers an uninterrupted view of the interior. By this time the shop had converted to self-service. Note the large number of pushchairs and infants left unattended outside. This branch shut in 1968.

Cambridge Dairy, No. 91 Kentish Town Road, 1904. Many London dairies were run by Welshmen, but despite his name, the owner of the Cambridge Dairy, Richard Davies, was born in St Pancras. His delivery carts and milk churns are parked outside. In 1901 three young milkmen were lodging with the Davies family.

This carefully-posed group photograph (including the dog on its hind legs!) was taken around 1906. Henry Merralls & Son, farriers, had a workshop behind No. 63 Fortess Rd from 1903 to 1913. Farriers would shoe horses and act as makeshift vets. In 1902, the number of horses in the UK was estimated at $3\frac{1}{2}$ million!

Hetty Scott's vegetable stall outside J. Sainsbury, 159 Queens Crescent, *c.* 1914. John Sainsbury opened this shop in 1873, the first of three in the road. Until about 1886, his family lived in the rooms above. Hetty regularly sent her daughter to buy milk at the shop.

J. Sainsbury, No. 159 Queens Crescent, *c.* 1913. With its shops and daily market, Queens Crescent was (and still is) a busy shopping street. The three Sainsbury shops in the road were competitive; assistants traded from the open shop windows as well as market tables, 'barking' or shouting to advertise their goods. This branch closed in 1962.

George Goodyear's off license, 91 Torriano Avenue, *c.* 1913. The advertising shows the shop was an agent for Ushers, a brewers based in Trowbridge, with a London brewery in Bayswater. George's wife Mary sent this postcard to her mother-in-law. She noted the 'ghost' dog, called Jim and belonging to her son Syd, that moved while the photo was being taken.

George Albert Cheeseman, milk contractor, No. 31 Oak Village, 1920. The firm traded as 'Lincolnshire Dairies', which was advertised on the carts and churns. The Cheesemans lived locally for many years. In 1881 the family had a dairy in Hanover Street near Queens Crescent; son George moved round the corner to Dale Road and later Oak Village. The business appears to have closed in the 1930s.

The splendidly bewhiskered gentleman is St Pancras-born Edwin Cossor. He is pictured in 1902 outside his bookbinder's and newsagent's shop at 12 Castle Road. One of the neighbourhood's longest-established businesses, Cossor traded at this address for over forty years. Directories show a furniture business had replaced him by 1917. The site has since been redeveloped.

The end wall of No. 1, Kentish Town Road, in February 1903. There are several layers of adverts, including fliers from the previous Christmas' entertainment at local venues: *Ali Baba* at the Bedford and *Aladdin* starring Harry Randall at the Camden Theatre. Randall was a well-known comedian on the halls and in pantomime. Perhaps the most unusual advert is for the Palace Hotel at Caux, Switzerland.

Twelve

On the Move

Entrance to locomotive engine shed, Camden Town, May 1839. This was one of a series of sketches by J.C. Bourne, depicting the building of the London and Birmingham Railway. This fire-proof shed, designed by Robert Stephenson, covered three quarters of an acre, with offices to register the arrival and departure of engines, plus a repair workshop. Engine 32 was built in Liverpool and cost upwards of £1,250. The railway attracted many sightseers, and one recalled: 'The trains were a new and amusing sight. I remember that a timid relation feared the engines would leave the line and career about Haverstock Hill in a deadly manner.'

The Regent's Canal opened in 1820, linking the Grand Junction Canal at Paddington to the Limehouse Docks. This branch bordered Albert Road, running through Park Village East and West to Cumberland Basin and Market, south of the Barracks. In 1942-43 it was infilled and the market later redeveloped as a housing estate. But once a year, a horse was walked along the dry canal bed, to assert the company's ownership.

Gloucester Gate Bridge, looking along the canal towards Regents Park Zoo, during rebuilding in 1877. Opened in August, it replaced the original 1814 bridge, which was too narrow and impeded traffic flow. This view no longer exists; although the bridge still stands, its original function is now redundant, as the canal below has been infilled.

The rebuilding of Camden Lock and Chalk Farm Road bridge, 1876-1877, looking east. The original 1815 brick bridge was collapsing under increased road traffic and only allowed one canal boat through at a time. The new bridge was opened in May 1877. Although it attracted general praise, the vestry surveyor was critical, describing its 'intense ugliness'. For him, the problem lay with the bridge's peculiar construction. Increasing the span over the canal from 20ft to 50ft meant using girders, parts of which projected above the level of the road, dividing it in two (see page 124).

The site of Camden Town Underground station, *c.* 1903, at the junction of Camden High Street and Kentish Town Road. The remarkable building on the left was nicknamed the 'cows' cathedral' after its elaborate gothic exterior. Claimed to be established in 1790, the dairy was certainly here from 1822. Cows used to graze the Kentish Town fields before they were built over, and were later kept in brick sheds behind the dairy. When the property was purchased for the site of the Underground station, Browns moved to Parkway in December 1903.

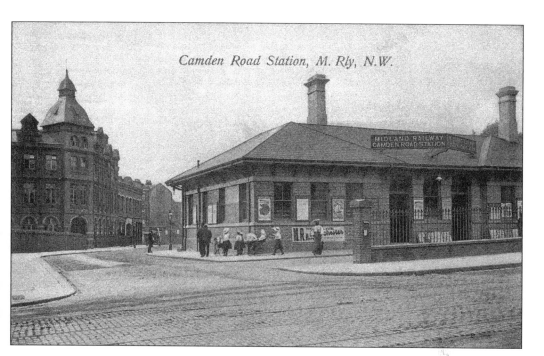

Camden Road station on the Midland Railway line, c. 1905. Situated on the corner of Sandall and Camden Roads, this station was convenient for pupils of North London Collegiate School, the substantial building in the background. The station closed in 1916, the victim of declining passenger numbers and wartime economies. A car dealership stands on the site today.

Looking northeast up Camden Road towards Camden Town station on the North London Railway (now Silverlink), c. 1905. Trains ran west to Kew and Richmond or east to Poplar, with a fourteen-minute journey to the City at Broad Street. Designed by Edwin Horne, the Italianate-style station dates from 1870. Today the ornamental roof ironwork is missing.

The Roundhouse, Chalk Farm, 1847, soon after opening. The functional, circular design by Robert Benson Dockray was deliberate, to accommodate a central turntable for moving engines from track to track, twenty-four in all, but it was soon made redundant, mainly due to increased engine size. Subsequent long-term use was as a bonded warehouse for Gilbeys the distillers. Since the 1960s, it has housed various arts and performance projects. The renovated building opened in 2006 as an arts venue managed by the Roundhouse Trust, and offering creative programmes for the 11-25s. The building is Grade II listed.

Looking towards Camden Town from the Roundhouse at Chalk Farm, across the London & Birmingham Railway lines, *c.* 1855. The steam engine in the foreground was a Stephenson 'Patentee' design, with a 'gothic' top to the firebox, which was seen on many of his locomotives.

Pickford's Depot, Oval Road, Camden Town, a lithograph by Thomas Allom. Opened in 1840/41, the building was arranged on several levels in order to handle goods by road, canal and railway. By 1846, Pickford's tonnage accounted for almost one tenth of the annual goods traffic of the London to Birmingham Railway. Rebuilt after a fire in 1857, Gilbeys later took over the depot and redeveloped the site.

Albert Road, *c.* 1900, looking towards St Mark's Church. The horse bus ran to Bayswater, hence the sign in the window, 'to and from Whitleys', Whitleys' being a large department store in Westbourne Grove. This official route replaced a short-lived 'shopping bus' service between Camden Town and Bayswater, provided by shop-owner William Whitley and his neighbours to encourage customers to visit their stores.

Chalk Farm Road canal bridge, *c.* 1905, showing the girder dividing the road after the new bridge was built. Camden Lock is to the left. The sender of the postcard described tyre problems on his bicycle journey from Dunstable to Kentish Town: 'I had to blow them up fresh; about every 4 or 5 minutes I had the same treat, it was a slow puncture!'

South Kentish Town underground station, Kentish Town Road, 1967. Still standing, this station opened in 1907 and struggled with low passenger numbers before shutting in 1924. In 1951, John Betjeman broadcast the story of 'Basil Green', who accidentally gets off at the closed station and has to be rescued by railway staff. However, it's unlikely that such an incident occurred.

The first motor tour made by the Chalk Farm Salvation Army band in 1911, when they visited Yorkshire and the Midlands. Pictured outside the Army's trade headquarters in Judd Street, the band started touring in 1902. Trips at home and abroad soon became an established part of their annual programme.

A 'Vanguard' bus shortly after the 24 route began running in May 1910, from Hampstead through Camden Town to Victoria. This is one of the longest-lived lines, and follows the same route today. The advertisement is for *Dame Nature*, starring Ethel Irving, a very popular actress who also produced the play at the Garrick Theatre in 1910.

Hampstead tram depot, Cressy Road, 1938. Rebuilt when horse-power was replaced by electricity, the depot served a small number of routes, running to South End Green and Parliament Hill Fields. Car 532 advertises Service 7, which ran between the Fields and Holborn. The depot was demolished in 1994 and the site redeveloped as offices and housing.

South End Green, 1909-10, soon after the line had been electrified. Mr J. Pearce is standing at the controls of his tram, waiting to depart for Tottenham Court Road, via Chalk Farm Road and Camden Town. He had worked on the line since 1899. The main advert on the tram's side is for a sale at Beddall's drapery shop in Kentish Town.

A No. 169 bus outside the Britannia pub, at the junction of Park Street with Camden High Street, in the 1930s. Park Street, renamed Parkway in 1937, then carried two-way traffic. The 169 started running in 1925, from Kilburn to Camden Town, Waterloo and Norwood, but the northern terminus was soon changed to Swiss Cottage. From 1928 the route linked Chalk Farm with Camden Town via Regent's Park Road and Delancey Street (southbound) and Park Street (northbound). But when the 169 was replaced by the 68A in October 1939, the new route abandoned Parkway and Regent's Park Road in favour of the main Chalk Farm Road.

Printed in Great Britain
by Amazon

50562325R00075